Favourite Poems We Learned in School

Chosen and Introduced
by
Thomas F Walsh

MERCIER PRESS

Mercier Press,
PO Box 5, 5 French Church Street, Cork
16 Hume Street, Dublin 2

© Introduction & Selection, Thomas F. Walsh

A CIP record for this book is available from the British Library.

ISBN 1 85635 051 7

10 9 8 7 6 5 4

FOR CAROLINE

Printed in Ireland by Colour Books Ltd.

Contents

Sweet Sorrow 75

Years of Exile 89

Love of Country 103

Introduction

One of my earliest recollections is listening to my mother quote from a poem about a fantastic island that lay to the west of Ireland:

> Men thought it a region of sunshine and rest,
> And they called it Hy-Brazil, the Isle of the Blest.

She could quote the whole poem from beginning to end, word-perfect. It is hard to convey the sense of pleasure it gave me, years later, to find the poem (by Gerald Griffin), in an old 1921 edition of a school-reader which I had rescued from the dusty book-bin of a small country school. I knew she had learned it from just such a book, 'off by heart', as we used to say. Another fine old lady, sadly no longer with us, recited 'The Burial of Sir John Moore' verbatim with a grand dignity, exactly as she had been taught to say it seventy years earlier.

These people were not by any means unique in this respect. When our grandparents and parents learned poetry, they always committed it to memory, and their retention was good; there was no bombardment from the demons of the electronic age. Such learning enriched their lives as well as their speech. Not only were they adept at finding the apt phrase, the relevant quotation, but, more importantly, the truths and values contained in these poems stayed with them while they lived and were passed on to new generations.

Nowadays there is a new approach to poetry in schools. There is not as much emphasis on learning as there is on experiencing the poem itself. I cannot help feeling that something has been lost. The recitation of poetry, like the art of storytelling, was something that was eminently suitable to the Celtic spirit, and was bound up, I feel, with the lyricism of our speech and the vividness of our imagination. But, I suppose, 'the old order changeth, yielding place to new', as the poet says, 'lest one good custom should corrupt the world'.

Through twenty-five years in Irish classrooms, both city and rural, I have put together a collection of what I think are the most quoted and the most memorable of the poems we learned in school in Ireland long ago. They were written a long time ago; the poets who wrote them, with one or two exceptions, have long since passed on, but the poems in this little book will remain with us until we too reach the end of our journey, mainly because we learned them when we were young, and consequently they have become part of us.

I do not claim for a moment that the poems in this book have great literary merit; some are good and some are not so good, but they have a few things in common. They were written by Irish poets (Joyce Kilmer claimed he was half Irish, and that is good enough for me!), they have a distinctly Irish flavour, and they all have appeared in National School textbooks at one time or another since the turn of the century. It is said of the Irish that 'all our wars were merry and all our songs were sad'; it is no surprise, then, that many of the poems here are patriotic and that there are a good number of sad ones too. The sadness of emigration, the joy of coming home, the memories of a childhood long passed, the unquenchable pride in one's country; these are the themes you will find here.

The poems are evocative, they stir a nostalgic chord, and they will bring you back to what many of us see as a better time.

I was prompted to put this collection into print by the number of times during my life as a teacher that people approached me with a time-worn quotation and wished to know who the poet was, or the title of the poem, or where they could find it. Well, here they are, all (I hope!) in one book, from the epic to the childish rhyme, all the poems that have stood the test of time, mainly because we learned them 'off by heart'!

At the back of the book you will find an Index of first lines which will help you find your particular favourite. I hope you enjoy reading the book as much as I have enjoyed putting it together.

T F WALSH

Memories

The Chapel on the Hill

The chapel of my childhood
Is on the green hillside,
And in the long grass up the hill
The graves of them that's died.

My mother often took me
When I was young and small,
I'd kneel upon her skirt and count
The Stations on the wall.

Each evening in the Maytime
The Rosary we'd say;
You'd hear beyond the chapel wall
The corncrakes in the hay.

The flowers round the altar,
They made the air smell sweet,
And cool the chapel floor would be
To little children's feet.

It's scarce a day was passing
But there I'd be awhile;
I mind the way the boys' bare feet
Went patting up the aisle.

The girls would come from lessons,
And kneel to say a prayer,
You'd see the noonday sunshine caught
In Mary Connor's hair.

Winifred M Letts

14

I will go with my Father

I will go with my father a-ploughing
To the green field by the sea,
And the rooks and the crows and the seagulls
Will come flocking after me.
I will sing to the patient horses
With the lark in the white of the air,
And my father will sing the plough-song
That blesses the cleaving share.

I will go with my father a-sowing
To the red field by the sea,
And the rooks and the gulls and the starlings
Will come flocking after me.
I will sing to the striding sowers
With the finch on the flowering sloe,
And my father will sing the seed-song
That only the wise men know.

I will go with my father a-reaping
To the brown field by the sea,
And the geese and the crows and the children
Will come flocking after me.
I will sing to the weary reapers
With the wren in the heat of the sun,
And my father will sing the scythe-song
That joys for the harvest done.

Joseph Campbell

The Little Waves of Breffny

The grand road from the mountain goes shining to the
    sea,
And there is traffic on it and many a horse and cart,
But the little roads of Cloonagh are dearer far to me,
And the little roads of Cloonagh go rambling through
    my heart.

A great storm from the ocean goes shouting o'er the
    hill,
And there is glory in it and terror on the wind,
But the haunted air of twilight is very strange and still,
And the little winds of twilight are dearer to my mind.

The great waves of the Atlantic sweep storming on the
    way,
Shining green and silver with the hidden herring shoal,
But the Little Waves of Breffny have drenched my
    heart in spray,
And the Little Waves of Breffny go stumbling through
    my soul.

Eva Gore-Booth

The Farmer's Son

Where'er are scattered the Irish nation,
In foreign lands or on Irish ground,
In every calling and rank and station
Good men and true will be always found:
But 'midst their masses
And ranks and classes,
When noble work must be dared and done,

No heart's more ready,
No hand's more steady
Than the heart and hand of a farmer's son.
His homely garb has not fashion's graces,
But it wraps a frame that is lithe and strong;
His brawny hand may show labour's traces,
But 'tis honest toil that does no man wrong.
For generous greeting,
For social meeting,
For genial mirth or for harmless fun,
'Midst high or low men,
'Midst friend or foemen,
Oh, where's the match for a farmer's son?

T D Sullivan

When You Are Old

When you are old and grey and full of sleep,
And nodding by the fire, take down this book,
And slowly read, and dream of the soft look
Your eyes had once, and of their shadows deep;

How many loved your moments of glad grace,
And loved your beauty with love false or true;
But one man loved the pilgrim soul in you,
And loved the sorrows of your changing face;

And bending down beside the glowing bars,
Murmur, a little sadly, how love fled
And paced upon the mountains overhead
And hid the face amid a crowd of stars.

W B Yeats

A Cradle Song

O men from the fields!
Come gently within.
Tread softly, softly,
O! men coming in.

Mavourneen is going
From me and from you,
Where Mary will fold him
With mantle of blue!

From reek of the smoke
And cold of the floor,
And the peering of things
Across the half-door.

O, men from the fields!
Soft, softly come thro'.
Mary puts round him
Her mantle of blue.

Padraic Colum

My Old Home

A poor old cottage tottering to its fall,
Some faded rose-trees scattered o'er the wall;
Four wooden pillars all slant one way,
A plot in front, bright green amid decay,
Where my wee pets, whene'er they came to tea,
Laughed, danced and played, and shouted in high
    glee;
A rusty paling and a broken gate

Shut out the world and bounded my estate.

Dusty and damp within, and rather bare,
Chokeful of books, here, there and everywhere.
Old-fashioned windows, and old doors that creaked,
Old ceilings cracked and grey, old walls that leaked.
Old chairs and tables, and an ancient lady
Worked out in tapestry, all rather shady.
Bright pictures in gilt frames, the only colour,
Making the grimy papering look duller.

What was the charm, the glamour that o'erspread
That dingy house and made it dear? – the dead.
The dead, the gentle, loving, kind and sweet,
The truest, tenderest heart that ever beat;
While she was with me 'twas indeed a *home*
Where every friend was welcome, when they'd come;
Her soft eyes shone with gladness, and her grace
Refined and beautified the poor old place.

But she is gone who made home for me there,
Whose child-like laugh, whose light step on the stair
Filled me with joy and gladness, hope and cheer,
To heaven she soared, and left me lonely here –
The old house now has got a brand-new face.
The roses are uprooted, there's no trace
Of broken laugh, or blossom – no decay –
The past is dead, the world wags on alway.

Ellen O'Leary

Those Evening Bells

Those evening bells! those evening bells!
How many a tale their music tells
Of youth and home, and that sweet time
When last I heard their soothing chime!

Those joyous hours are passed away
And many a heart, that then was gay,
Within the tomb now darkly dwells
And hears no more those evening bells!

And so 'twill be when I am gone!
That tuneful peal will still ring on,
While other bards shall walk these dells,
And sing your praise, sweet evening bells!

Thomas Moore

Four Ducks on a Pond

Four ducks on a pond,
A grass-bank beyond,
A blue sky of spring,
White clouds on the wing:
What a little thing
To remember for years –
To remember with tears!

William Allingham

Danny Murphy

He was as old as old can be,
His little eyes could scarcely see,
His mouth was sunken in between
His nose and chin, and he was lean
And twisted up and withered quite
So that he couldn't walk aright.

His pipe was always going out,
And then he'd have to search about
In all his pockets, and he'd mow
– O, deary me! and, musha now!
And then he'd light his pipe, and then
He'd let it go clean out again.

He couldn't dance or jump or run,
Or ever have a bit of fun
Like me and Susan, when we shout
And jump and throw ourselves about:
– But when he laughed, then you could see
He was as young as young could be!

James Stephens

By the Fireside

Where glows the Irish hearth with peat
There lives a subtle spell –
The faint blue smoke, the gentle heat,
The moorland odours, tell

Of long roads running through a red
Untamed unfurrowed land,

With curlews keening overhead,
And streams on either hand;

Black turf-banks crowned with whispering sedge,
And black bog-pools below;
While dry stone wall or ragged ledge
Leads on, to meet the glow

From cottage doors, that lure us in
From rainy western skies,
To seek the friendly warmth within,
The simple talk and wise;

Or tales of magic and of arms
From days when princes met
To listen to the lay that charms
The Connacht dweller yet.

And still around the fires of peat
Live on the ancient days;
There still do living lips repeat
The old and deathless lays.

And when the wavering wreaths ascend,
Blue in the evening air,
The soul of Ireland seems to bend
Above her children there.

T W Rolleston

The Wintry Night

Around the fire, one wintry night,
The farmer's rosy children sat,
The faggot lent its cheerful light,
And jokes went round, and harmless chat.

When hark! a gentle hand they hear
Low tapping at the bolted door;
And, thus to gain their willing ear,
A feeble voice was heard implore.

'Cold blows the blast across the moor,
The sleet drives hissing in the wind;
Yon toilsome mountain lies before,
A dreary, treeless waste behind.

'My eyes are weak and dim with age,
No road, no path, can I descry;
And these poor rags ill stand the rage
Of such a keen, inclement sky.

'So faint am I, these tottering feet
No more my palsied frame can bear;
My freezing heart forgets to beat,
And drifting snows my tomb prepare.

'Open your hospitable door,
And shield me from the biting blast;
Cold, cold it blows across the moor,
The weary moor that I have passed!'

With hasty steps the farmer ran,
And close before the fire they place
The poor half-frozen beggar man,
With shaking limbs and pallid face.

The little children flocking came,
And warmed his stiffened hands in theirs
And busily the kindly dame
A comfortable meal prepares.

Their welcome cheered his drooping soul;
And slowly down his wrinkled cheek,
The big round tear was seen to roll,
That told the thanks he could not speak.

The children, too, began to sigh,
And all their merry chat was o'er;
And yet they felt – they knew not why –
More glad than they had been before.

Anonymous

A Child's World

Irish Children

Happy Irish children,
In your home below,
Sheltered when the rain falls,
Safe from winter's snow.

Sing your songs of gladness
In your grand old speech,
Climb the sunny hillside,
Race along the beach.

Nowhere greener pastures,
Nowhere browner hills,
Nowhere bluer rivers
Fed by sparkling rills.

This is holy Ireland
Where our fathers trod,
This is the land where Patrick
Told them first of God.

Love her, do not leave her,
O'er the world to roam;
Ireland needs her children –
Work for her at home.

An Dara-Leabhar
(Gaelic League)

If I Knew

If I knew the box where the smiles are kept,
No matter how large the key,
Or strong the bolt I would try so hard
'Twould open I know for me,
Then over the land and sea broadcast
I'd scatter the smiles to play,
That the children's faces might hold them fast
For many and many a day.

If I knew the box that was large enough
To hold all the frowns I meet,
I would like to gather them every one
From the nursery, school or street,
Then, folding and holding, I'd pack them in
And turning the monster key,
I'd hire a giant to drop the box
To the depths of the deep, deep sea.

Anonymous

My Mother

Who fed me from her gentle breast,
And hushed me in her arms to rest,
And on my cheek sweet kisses prest?
　　　　　My Mother.

When sleep forsook my open eye,
Who was it sung sweet lullaby,
And rocked me that I should not cry?
　　　　　My Mother.

Who sat and watched my infant head,
When sleeping in my cradle bed,
And tears of sweet affection shed?
    My Mother.

When pain and sickness made me cry,
Who gazed upon my heavy eye,
And wept for fear that I should die?
    My Mother.

Who ran to help me when I fell,
And would some pretty story tell,
Or kiss the part to make it well?
    My Mother.

Who taught my infant lips to pray,
To love God's holy word and day,
And walk in wisdom's pleasant way?
    My Mother.

And can I ever cease to be
Affectionate and kind to thee,
Who was so very kind to me?
    My Mother.

Oh, no! the thought I cannot bear,
And, if God please my life to spare,
I hope I shall reward thy care,
    My Mother.

When thou art feeble, old and grey,
My healthy arm shall be thy stay,
And I will soothe thy pains away,
    My Mother.

And when I see thee hang thy head,
'Twill be my turn to watch thy bed,

And tears of sweet affection shed,
    My Mother.

Anonymous

A Noble Boy

The woman was old, and feeble, and grey,
And bent with the chill of the winter's day;
The street was wet with the recent snow,
And the woman's feet were weary and slow.
She stood at the crossing, and waited long,
Alone, uncared for, amid the throng.
Down the street, with laughter and shout,
Glad in the freedom of 'school let out',
Came the boys, like a flock of sheep;
Hailing the snow, piled white and deep.
Past the woman, so old and grey,
Hastened the children on their way,
Nor offered a helping hand to her,
So meek, so timid, afraid to stir.

At last came one of the merry troop –
The gayest boy of all the group;
He paused beside her, and whispered low,
'I'll help you across if you wish to go';
He guided the trembling feet along,
Proud, that his own were firm and strong.
Then back again to his friends, he went,
His young heart happy, and well content,
'She is somebody's mother, boys, you know,
Although she is old, and poor and slow.
And I hope some fellow will lend a hand
To help my mother – you understand –
If e'er she be poor, and old and grey,
When her own dear boy is far away.'

And 'somebody's mother' bowed low her head,
In her home that night, and the prayer she said
Was, 'God be kind to the noble boy,
Who is somebody's son, and pride, and joy.'

Anonymous

Timothy Dan

Timothy Dan
Is a very rich man,
And he keeps all his wealth in his pockets:
Four buttons, a box,
The keys of two clocks,
And the chain of his grandmother Margaret's
        locket.
A big piece of string
(It's a most useful thing),
A watch without hands,
And three rubber bands,
Five glassy marbles,
Some tail-ends of chalk,
A squeaker that once
Made a golliwog talk,
A broken-down penknife
With only one blade,
And a little toy boat
That his grandfather made.

You'd never believe
(Hearing such a long list)
That there's room in each pocket
For one little fist;
You'd never believe
That the smallest of boys

Could carry so much
In his wee corduroys.

John D Sheridan

Mr Nobody

I know a funny little man,
As quiet as a mouse,
Who does the mischief that is done
In everybody's house.
Though no one ever sees his face,
Yet we can all agree
That every plate we break was cracked
By Mr Nobody.

'Tis he who always tears our books,
Who leaves the door ajar,
Who pulls the buttons from our shirts,
And scatters pins afar;
That squeaking door will always squeak
For – this is plain to see –
We leave the oiling to be done
By Mr Nobody.

'Tis he who brings in all the mud
That gathers in the hall.
'Tis he who lets the front-door slam,
And scribbles on the wall.
When we can't find the scissors,
Or have lost the back-door key,
The one to blame in every case
Is Mr Nobody.

We know he cracked the window,
And broke the china plate,

We know he left the kitchen floor
In such a dreadful state.
We know his faults and failings,
His sins are plain to see,
And so we always put the blame
On Mr Nobody.

Anonymous

Do What You Do

Drive the nail aright, boys,
Hit it on the head;
Strike with all your might, boys,
While the iron's red.

When you've work to do, boys,
Do it with a will;
They who reach the top, boys,
First must climb the hill.

Standing at the foot, boys,
Gazing at the sky,
How can you get up, boys,
If you never try?

Though you stumble oft, boys,
Never be down-cast;
Try, and try again, boys –
You'll succeed at last.

From an old reader (1921)
by the Christian Brothers

The Comical Child

Have you heard about Marigold,
The girl who was young before she was old?

Just over her mouth was an elegant nose,
And inside her slippers she carried ten toes.

And (this is what really made people stare)
The top of her head was covered with hair.

People who knew her from childhood have said
That she fell fast asleep every night in her bed.

Moreover – and this must occasion tremendous
        surprise –
When sleeping she always shut tight *both* her eyes.

She could be cross, and she could be mild –
Mercy me! What a comical child!

And let me say this with the fullest authority
Her real name was Marigold, *not* Mary Dorothy.

For I'm speaking of Marigold, this is quite plain,
And not of Lucinda, or Noreen, or Jane.

Anonymous

Sycamore Tree

Sycamore tree, sycamore tree,
How did you grow so tall?
Up into the blue sky,

Beside the garden wall;
Right up to the nursery window,
As big as a tree can be –
It must have taken you years and years,
Sycamore, sycamore tree.

Sycamore tree, sycamore tree,
How did you grow so tall?
I know you weren't *always* big,
That once you were *ever* so small;
Scarce up to the scullery window,
And now you're as big as can be –
It must have taken you years and years,
Sycamore, sycamore tree.

John D Sheridan

The Song of Wandering Aengus

I went out to the hazel wood,
Because a fire was in my head,
And cut and peeled a hazel wand,
And hooked a berry to a thread;
And when white moths were on the wing,
And moth-like stars were flickering out,
I dropped the berry in a stream
And caught a little silver trout.

When I had laid it on the floor
I went to blow the fire aflame,
But something rustled on the floor,
And some one called me by my name:
It had become a glimmering girl
With apple blossom in her hair
Who called me by my name and ran
And faded through the brightening air.

Though I am old with wandering
Through hollow lands and hilly lands,
I will find out where she is gone,
And kiss her lips and take her hands;
And walk among long dappled grass,
And pluck till time and times are done
The silver apples of the moon,
The golden apples of the sun.

W B Yeats

The Fairies
(A Child's Song)

Up the airy mountain
Down the rushy glen,
We daren't go a hunting
For fear of little men;
Wee folk, good folk,
Trooping all together;
Green jacket, red cap,
And white owl's feather.

Down along the rocky shore
Some make their home –
They live on crispy pancakes
Of yellow tide-foam;
Some in the reeds
Of the black mountain lake,
With frogs for their watch-dogs,
All night awake.

By the craggy hill-side,
Through the mosses bare,
They have planted thorn trees

For pleasure here and there.
Is any man so daring
As dig one up in spite,
He shall find their sharpest thorns
In his bed at night.

Up the airy mountain,
Down the rushy glen,
We daren't go a-hunting
For fear of little men;
Wee folk, good folk,
Trooping all together;
Green jacket, red cap,
And white owl's feather!

William Allingham

And Then I Remembered

Mum tucked me in,
And said my prayers,
And then I heard her
Go down the stairs.

I felt so lonely,
Lying here,
With no one to talk to,
And nobody near.

And then I remembered,
As here I lay,
Someone who never
Goes away;

Somebody big,
And Somebody small,

Who made the world,
And the heavens all;

Who lit the stars
In the dark blue air,
And gave the daffodil
Clothes to wear;

Someone who once
Was a child like me,
When Mary fondled Him
On her knee.

So I remembered,
As here I lay,
Someone who never
Goes away;

Somebody big,
And Somebody small –
And I wasn't lonely,
At all, at all.

John D Sheridan

Little by Little

'Little by Little,' an acorn said,
As it slowly sank in its mossy bed,
'I am improving every day,
Hidden deep in the earth away.'

Little by little each day it grew,
Little by little it sipped the dew;
Downward it sent a thread-like root,
Up in the air sprang a tiny shoot.

Day after day, and year after year,
Little by little the leaves appear;
And the slender branches spread far and wide,
Till the mighty oak is the forest's pride.

'Little by little,' said a thoughtful boy,
'Each precious moment I will employ,
And always this rule in my mind shall dwell:
Whatever I do, I'll do it well.

'Little by little, I'll learn to know
The treasured wisdom of long ago;
And sometime, perhaps, the world will be
Happier and better because of me.'

Anonymous

Nature's Child

Nature's Child

Still south I went, and west, and south again,
Through Wicklow from the morning to the night,
And far from cities and the sights of men,
Lived with the sunshine and the moon's delight.

I knew the stars, the flowers and the birds,
The grey and wintry sides of many glens,
And did but half remember human words,
In converse with the mountains, moors and fens.

J M Synge

All Things Bright and Beautiful

All things bright and beautiful,
All creatures great and small,
All things wise and wonderful,
The Lord God made them all.

Each little flower that opens,
Each little bird that sings,
He made their glowing colours,
He made their tiny wings.

The rich man in his castle,
The poor man at his gate,
God made them high or lowly,
And ordered their estate.

The purple-headed mountain,
The river running by,
The sunset and the morning,

That brightens up the sky;

The cold wind in the winter,
The pleasant summer sun,
The ripe fruits in the garden –
He made them every one.

The tall trees in the greenwood,
The meadows where we play,
The rushes by the water
We gather every day;

He gave us eyes to see them,
And lips that we might tell,
How great is God Almighty,
Who has made all things well.

Cecil Frances Alexander

The Presence of God

I see His blood upon the rose,
And in the stars the glory of His eyes;
His body gleams amid eternal snows,
His tears fall from the skies.

I see His face in every flower;
The thunder, and the singing of the birds
Are but His voice; and, carven by His power,
Rocks are His written words.

All pathways by His feet are worn;
His strong heart stirs the ever-beating sea;
His crown of thorns is twined with every thorn;
His cross is every tree.

Joseph Mary Plunkett

Frolic

The children were shouting together
And racing along the sands,
A glimmer of dancing shadows,
A dove-like flutter of hands.

The stars were shouting in heaven,
The sun was chasing the moon.
The game was the same as the children's,
They danced to the self-same tune.

The whole of the world was merry,
One joy from vale to height,
Where the blue woods of twilight encircled
The lovely lawns of the light.

'A E' – *George Russell*

Birds' Nests

The skylark's nest among the grass
And waving corn is found;
The robin's on a shady bank,
With oak leaves strewn around.

The wren builds in an ivied thorn
Or old and ruined wall;
The mossy nest so covered in,
You scarce can see at all.

The martins build their nests of clay,
In rows beneath the eaves;
While silvery lichens, moss and hair,

The chaffinch interweaves.

The cuckoo makes no nest at all,
But through the wood she strays
Until she finds one snug and warm,
And there her egg she lays.

The sparrow has a nest of hay,
With feathers warmly lined;
The ring-dove's careless nest of sticks
On lofty trees we find.

Rooks build together in a wood,
And often disagree;
The owl will build inside a barn
Or in a hollow tree.

The blackbird's nest of grass and mud
In brush and bank is found;
The lapwing's darkly spotted eggs
Are laid upon the ground.

The magpie's nest is girt with thorns
In leafless tree or hedge;
The wild duck and the water-hen
Build by the water's edge.

Birds build their nests from year to year,
According to their kind,
Some very neat and beautiful
Some easily designed.

Anonymous

White Fields

In the winter time we go
Walking in the fields of snow,
Where there is no grass at all;
Where the top of every wall,.
Every fence, and every tree,
Is as white as white can be.

Pointing out the way we came
– Every one of them the same –
All across the fields there be
Prints in silver filigree;
And our mothers always know,
By the footprints in the snow,
Where it is the children go.

James Stephens

Trees

I think that I shall never see
A poem lovely as a tree.

A tree whose hungry mouth is prest
Against the earth's sweet flowing breast;

A tree that looks at God all day,
And lifts her leafy arms to pray;

A tree that may in Summer wear
A nest of robins in her hair;

Upon whose bosom snow has lain;
Who intimately lives with rain.

Poems were made by fools like me,
But only God can make a tree.

Robin Redbreast

Goodbye, goodbye to Summer!
For Summer's nearly done;
The garden smiling faintly,
Cool breezes in the sun;
Our thrushes now are silent,
Our swallows flown away –
But Robin's here in coat of brown
With ruddy breast-knot gay.
Robin, Robin Redbreast,
O, Robin dear!
Robin singing sweetly
In the falling year.

Bright yellow, red and orange,
The leaves come down in hosts;
The trees are Indian Princes,
But soon they'll turn to Ghosts;
The scanty pears and apples
Hang russet on the bough;
It's Autumn, Autumn, Autumn late
'Twill soon be Winter now.
Robin, Robin Redbreast,
O, Robin dear!
And welladay! my Robin,
For pinching times are near.

The fireside for the Cricket,
The wheatstack for the Mouse
When trembling night-winds whistle
And moan all round the house;
The frosty ways like iron,
The branches plumed with snow –
Alas! in Winter, dead and dark,
Where can poor Robin go?
Robin, Robin Redbreast,
O, Robin dear!
And a crumb of bread for Robin,
His little heart to cheer.

William Allingham

The Star of Heaven

Shine on, thou bright beacon,
Unclouded and free,
From thy high place of calmness
O'er life's troubled sea;
Its morning of promise,
Its smooth waves are gone,
And the billows wave wildly –
Then, bright one, shine on.

The wings of the tempest
May rush o'er thy ray;
But tranquil thou smilest,
Undimmed by its sway;
High, high o'er the world
Where the storms are unknown,
Thou dwellest all beauteous,
All glorious – alone.

From the deep womb of darkness

The lightning flash leaps,
O'er the bark of my fortunes
Each mad billow sweeps;
From the port of her safety,
By warring winds driven,
And no light o'er her course
But you lone one of Heaven.

Yet fear not, thou frail one,
The hour may be near,
When our own sunny headland
Far off shall appear;
When the voice of the storm
Shall be silent and past,
In some island of Heaven
We may anchor at last.

J J Callanan

The North Wind Doth Blow

The north wind doth blow and we shall have snow,
And what will the robin do then, poor thing?
He'll sit in the barn and keep himself warm
And hide his head under his wing, poor thing!

The north wind doth blow and we shall have snow,
And what will the swallow do then, poor thing?
Oh, do you not know? He's gone long ago
To a land that is warmer than ours, poor thing!

The north wind doth blow and we shall have snow,
And what will the children do then, poor things?
When lessons are done they'll jump, skip and run,
And play till they keep themselves warm, poor things.

Old Rhyme

August Weather

Dead heat and windless air,
And silence over all;
Never a leaf astir,
But the ripe apples fall;
Plums are purple-red,
Pears amber and brown;
Thud! in the garden-bed
Ripe apples fall down.

Air like a cider-press
With the bruised apples' scent;
Low whistles express
Some sleepy bird's content;
Still world and windless sky,
A mist of heat o'er all,
Peace like a lullaby,
And the ripe apples fall.

Katherine Tynan

A Soft Day

A soft day, thank God!
A wind from the south
With a honeyed mouth;
A scent of drenching leaves,
Briar and beech and lime,
White elder-flower and thyme
And the soaking grass smells sweet,
Crushed by my two bare feet,
While the rain drips,
Drips, drips, drips from the eaves.

A soft day, thank God!
The hills wear a shroud
Of silver cloud;
The web the spider weaves
Is a glittering net;
The woodland path is wet,
And the soaking earth smells sweet
Under my two bare feet,
And the rain drips,
Drips, drips, drips from the leaves.

Winifred M Letts

The Snare

I hear a sudden cry of pain!
There is a rabbit in a snare:
Now I hear the cry again,
But I cannot tell from where.

But I cannot tell from where
He is calling out for aid!
Crying on the frightened air,
Making everything afraid!

Making everything afraid!
Wrinkling up his little face!
As he cries again for aid;
– And I cannot find the place!

And I cannot find the place
Where his paw is in the snare!
Little One! Oh, Little One!
I am searching everywhere!

James Stephens

A Drover

To Meath of the pastures,
From wet hills by the sea,
Through Leitrim and Longford,
Go my cattle and me.

I hear in the darkness
Their slipping and breathing –
I name them the by-ways
They're to pass without heeding;

Then the wet, winding roads,
Brown bogs with black water,
And my thoughts on white ships
And the King o' Spain's daughter.

O farmer, strong farmer!
You can spend at the fair,
But your face you must turn
To your crops and your care;

And soldiers, red soldiers!
You've seen many lands,
But you walk two by two
And by captain's commands!

O the smell of the beasts,
The wet wind in the morn,
And the proud and hard earth
Never broken for corn!

And the crowds at the fair,
The herds loosened and blind,
Loud words and dark faces,
And the wild blood behind!

(O strong men with your best
I would strive breast to breast,
I could quiet your herds
With my words, with my words!)

I will bring you, my kine,
Where there's grass to the knee,
But you'll think of scant croppings
Harsh with salt of the sea.

Padraic Colum

On the Silver Strand at Wicklow

Across the shining silver strand
I saw the golden sea;
The waves were laughing in the sun
And rolling up to me.

Then back they went, and on they came
And tumbled in the caves;
I think that I have never seen
Such happy things as waves.

Anonymous

Lines Addressed to a Seagull
seen off the Cliffs of Moher, in the County of Clare

White bird of the tempest! oh, beautiful thing,
With the bosom of snow, and the motionless wing,
Now sweeping the billow, now floating on high,
Now bathing thy plumes in the light of the sky,
Now poising o'er ocean thy delicate form,
Now breasting the surge with thy bosom so warm,
Now darting aloft, with a heavenly scorn,
Now shooting along like a ray of the morn;
Now lost in the folds of the cloud curtained dome,
Now floating abroad like a flake of the foam;
Now silently poised o'er the war of the main,
Like the spirit of charity brooding o'er pain;
Now gliding with pinion, all silently furled,
Like an angel descending to comfort the world.
Thou seem'st to my spirit, as upward I gaze –
And see thee, now clothed in mellowest rays,
Now lost in the storm-driven vapours that fly,
Like hosts that are routed across the broad sky –
Like a pure spirit true to its virtue and faith,
'Mid the tempests of nature, of passion, and death!
Rise! beautiful emblem of purity! rise
On the sweet winds of heaven, to thine own brilliant
       skies,
Still higher! still higher! 'till lost to our sight,
Thou hidest thy wings in a mantle of light;
And I think of a pure spirit gazing on thee,
Must long for the moment – the joyous and free –
When the soul, disembodied from nature, shall spring,
Unfettered, at once to her Maker and King;
When the bright day of service and suffering past,
Shapes, fairer than thine, shall shine round her last,
While the standard of battle triumphantly furled,

She smiles like a victor, serene on the world!

Gerald Griffin

Sheep and Lambs

All in the April evening,
April airs were abroad;
The sheep with their little lambs
Passed me by on the road.

The sheep with their little lambs
Passed me by on the road;
All in the April evening,
I thought on the Lamb of God.

The lambs were weary, and crying
With a weak, human cry.
I thought on the Lamb of God
Going meekly to die.

Up in the blue, blue mountains
Dewy pastures are sweet;
Rest for the little bodies,
Rest for the little feet.

But for the Lamb of God,
Up on the hill-top green,
Only a cross of shame,
Two stark crosses between.

All in the April evening,
April airs were abroad;
I saw the sheep with their lambs,
And thought on the Lamb of God.

Katherine Tynan

Calvary

There is a green hill far away
Without a city wall,
Where the dear Lord was crucified
Who died to save us all.

We may not know, we cannot tell
What pains He had to bear,
But we do know it was for us
He hung and suffered there.

He died that we might be forgiven,
He died to make us good,
That we might go at last to Heaven,
Saved by His Precious Blood.

There was none other good enough
To pay the price of sin;
He only could unlock the gate
Of Heaven and let us in.

O, dearly, dearly has He loved,
And we must love Him too
With all our strength and all our mind,
And prove our love is true.

C F Alexander

Evening Brings Us Home

Upon the hills the wind is sharp and cold;
The sweet young grasses wither on the wold;
And we, O Lord, have wandered from Thy fold;
But evening brings us home.

Among the mists we stumbled, and the rocks
Where the brown lichen whitens, and the fox
Watches the straggler from the scattered flocks;
But evening brings us home.

The sharp thorns pierce us, and our tender feet
Are cut and bleeding, and the lambs repeat
Their pitiful complaints: oh! rest is sweet
When evening brings us home.

We have been wounded by the hunter's darts;
Our eyes are very heavy, and our hearts
Search for Thy coming: when the light departs
At evening brings us home.

The darkness gathers. Through the gloom no star
Rises to guide us. We have wandered far.
Without Thy lamp we know not where we are;
At evening bring us home.

The clouds are round us and the snow-drifts
    thicken;
O Thou, dear Shepherd, leave us not to sicken
In the waste night: our tardy footsteps quicken;
At evening bring us home.

Anonymous

The Light of Other Days

The Light of Other Days

Oft in the stilly night
Ere slumber's chain has bound me,
Fond memory brings the light
Of other days around me:
The smiles, the tears
Of boyhood's years,
The words of love then spoken;
The eyes that shone,
Now dimmed and gone,
The cheerful hearts now broken!
Thus in the stilly night
Ere slumber's chain has bound me,
Sad memory brings the light
Of other days around me.

When I remember all
The friends so link'd together
I've seen around me fall
Like leaves in wintry weather,
I feel like one
Who treads alone
Some banquet-hall deserted,
Whose lights are fled,
Whose garlands dead
And all but he departed!
Thus in the stilly night
Ere slumber's chain has bound me,
Sad memory brings the light
Of other days around me.

Thomas Moore

The Dead at Clonmacnois

In a quiet water'd land, a land of roses,
Stands Saint Kieran's city fair:
And the warriors of Erin in their famous generations
Slumber there.

There beneath the dewy hillside sleep the noblest
Of the clann of Conn,
Each below his stone with name in branching Ogham
And the sacred knot thereon.

There they laid to rest the seven Kings of Tara,
There the sons of Cairbré sleep –
Battle-banners of the Gael, that in Kieran's plain of
      crosses
Now their final hosting keep.

And in Clonmacnois they laid the men of Teffia,
And right many a lord of Breagh;
Deep the sod above Clan Creidé and Clan Conaill,
Kind in hall and fierce in fray.

Many and many a son of Conn, the Hundred-Fighter,
In the red earth lies at rest;
Many a blue eye of Clan Colman the turf covers,
Many a swan-white breast.

T W Rolleston

59

The Paschal Fire of Patrick

On Tara's hill the daylight dies,
On Tara's plain 'tis dead.
"Till Baal's unkindled fires shall rise
No fire must flame instead.'

'Tis thus the King, commanding, speaks,
Commands and speaks in vain;
For lo! a fire defiant breaks
From out the woods of Slane.

For there, in prayer, is Patrick bent,
With Christ his soul is knit;
And there, before his simple tent,
The Paschal fire is lit.

'What means this flame that through the night
Illumines all the vale?
What rebel hand a fire dare light
Before the fires of Baal?'

O King! when Baal's dark reign is o'er,
When thou thyself art gone,
This fire will light the Irish shore
And lead its people on;

Will lead them on full many a night
Through which they're doomed to go,
Like that which led the Israelite
From bondage and from woe.

This fire, this sacred fire of God,
Young hearts shall bear afar
To lands no human foot hath trod,
Beneath the Western Star;

To lands where Faith's bright flag unfurled
By those who here have knelt
Shall give unto a newer world
The sceptre of the Celt.

D F McCarthy

Let Erin Remember the Days of Old

Let Erin remember the days of old,
Ere her faithless sons betrayed her;
When Malachi wore the collar of gold,
Which he won from her proud invader;
When her kings, with standard of green unfurled,
Led the Red-Branch Knights to danger; –
Ere the emerald gem of the western world
Was set in the crown of a stranger.

On Lough Neagh's bank as the fisherman strays,
When the clear cold eve's declining,
He sees the round towers of other days
In the wave beneath him shining;
Thus shall memory often, in dreams sublime,
Catch a glimpse of the days that are over;
Thus, sighing, look through the waves of time
For the long-faded glories they cover.

Thomas Moore

The Burial of King Cormac

'Crom Cruach and his sub-gods twelve,'
Said Cormac, 'are but carven treene;
The axe that made them, haft or helve,
Had worthier of our worship been.

'But He who made the tree to grow,
And hid in earth the iron-stone,
And made the man with mind to know
The axe's use, is God alone.'

Anon to priests of Crom was brought –
Where, girded in their service dread,
They ministered on red Moy Slaught –
Word of the words King Cormac said.

They loosed their curse against the king;
They cursed him in his flesh and bones;
And daily in their mystic ring
They turned the maledictive stones;

Till, where at meat the monarch sate,
Amid the revel and the wine,
He choked upon the food he ate,
At Sletty, southward of the Boyne.

High vaulted then the priestly throng,
And far and wide they noised abroad
With trump and loud liturgic song
The praise of their avenging God.

But ere the voice was wholly spent
That priest and prince should still obey,
To awed attendants o'er him bent
Great Cormac gathered breath to say –

'Spread not the beds of Brugh for me
When restless death-bed's use is done:
But bury me at Rosnaree
And face me to the rising sun.

'For all the kings who lie in Brugh
Put trust in gods of wood and stone;
And 'twas at Ross that first I knew
One, Unseen, Who is God alone.

'His glory lightens from the east;
His message soon shall reach our shore;
And idol-god, and cursing priest
Shall plague us from Moy Slaught no more.'

Dead Cormac on his bier they laid: –
'He reigned a king for forty years,
And shame it were,' his captains said,
'He lay not with his royal peers,'

'His grandsire, Hundred-Battle, sleeps
Serene in Brugh: and, all around,
Dead kings in stone sepulchral keeps
Protect the sacred burial ground.

'What though a dying man should rave
Of changes o'er the eastern sea?
In Brugh of Boyne shall be his grave,
And not in noteless Rosnaree.'

Then northward forth they bore the bier,
And down from Sletty side they drew,
With horsemen and with charioteer,
To cross the fords of Boyne to Brugh.

There came a breath of finer air
That touched the Boyne with ruffling wings,
It stirred him in his sedgy lair
And in his mossy moorland springs.

And as the burial train came down,
With dirge and savage dolorous shows,
Across their pathway, broad and brown
The deep full-hearted river rose;

From bank to bank through all his fords,
'Neath blackening squalls he swelled and boiled,
And thrice the wondering gentile lords
Essayed to cross, and thrice recoiled.

Then forth stepped grey-haired warriors four:
They said, 'Through angrier floods than these,
On linked shields once our king we bore
From Dread-Spear and the hosts of Deece.

'And long as loyal will holds good,
And limbs respond with helpful thews,
Nor flood, nor fiend within the flood,
Shall bar him of his burial dues.'

With slanted necks they stooped to lift;
They heaved him up to neck and chin:
And, pair and pair, with footsteps swift,
Locked arm and shoulder, bore him in.

'Twas brave to see them leave the shore;
To mark the deep'ning surges rise,
And fall subdued in foam before
The tension of their striding thighs.

'Twas brave, when now a spear cast-out,
Breast-high the battling surges ran;
For weight was great, and limbs were stout,
And loyal man put trust in man.

But ere they reached the middle deep,
Nor steadying weight of clay they bore,
Nor strain of sinewy limbs could keep
Their feet beneath the swerving four.

And now they slide, and now they swim,
And now, amid the blackening squall,
Grey locks afloat, with clutching grim,
They plunge around the floating pall.

While, as a youth with practised spear
Through jostling crowds bears off the ring,
Boyne from their shoulders caught the bier
And proudly bore away the king.

At morning on the grassy marge
Of Rosnaree the corpse was found,
And shepherds at their early charge
Entombed it in the peaceful ground.

A tranquil spot: a hopeful sound
Comes from the ever-youthful stream,
And still on daisied mead and mound
The dawn delays with tenderer beam.

Round Cormac Spring renews her buds;
In March perpetual by his side
Down come the earth-fresh April floods,
And up the sea-fresh salmon glide;

And life and time rejoicing run
From age to age their wonted way;
But still he waits the risen Sun,
For still 'tis only dawning Day.

Sir Samuel Ferguson

The Harp that Once through Tara's Halls

The harp that once through Tara's halls
The soul of music shed,
Now hangs as mute on Tara's walls
As if that soul was fled,
So sleeps the pride of former days,
So glory's thrill is o'er,
And hearts, that once beat high for praise,
Now feel that pulse no more.

No more to chiefs and ladies bright
The harp of Tara swells:
The chord alone, that breaks at night,
Its tale of ruin tells.
Thus Freedom now so seldom wakes,
The only throb she gives
Is when some heart indignant breaks,
To show that still she lives.

Thomas Moore

from The Deserted Village

Sweet Auburn! parent of the blissful hour,
Thy glades forlorn confess the tyrant's power.
Here, as I take my solitary rounds,
Amidst thy tangling walks, and ruined grounds,
And, many a year elapsed, return to view
Where once the cottage stood, the hawthorn grew,
Remembrance wakes, with all her busy train,
Swells at my breast, and turns the past to pain.
    In all my wanderings round this world of care,

In all my griefs – and God has given my share –
I still had hopes my latest hours to crown,
Amidst these humble bowers to lay me down;
To husband out life's taper at the close,
And keep the flame from wasting by repose:
I still had hopes, for pride attends us still,
Amidst the swains to show my book-learn'd skill,
Around my fire an evening group to draw,
And tell of all I felt, and all I saw;
And, as a hare whom hounds and horns pursue,
Pants to the place from whence at first he flew,
I still had hopes, my long vexations past,
Here to return – and die at home at last ...

Sweet was the sound, when oft, at evening's close,
Up yonder hill the village murmur rose;
There, as I passed with careless steps and slow,
The mingling notes came softened from below;
The swain responsive as the milk-maid young;
The noisy geese that gabbled o'er the pool,
The playful children just let loose from school;
The watch-dog's voice that bayed the whispering
          wind,
And the loud laugh that spoke the vacant mind;
These all in sweet confusion sought the shade,
And filled each pause the nightingale had made
But now the sounds of population fail,
No cheerful murmurs fluctuate in the gale;
No busy steps the grass-grown footway tread,
For all the bloomy flush of life is fled:
All but yon widowed, solitary thing,
That feebly bends beside the plashy spring;
She, wretched matron, forced in age, for bread,
To strip the brook with mantling cresses spread,
To pick her wintry faggot from the thorn,
To seek her nightly shed, and weep till morn;
She only left of all the harmless train,
The sad historian of the pensive plain.

Near yonder copse, where once the garden smiled,
And still where many a garden flower grows wild;
There, where a few torn shrubs the place disclose,
The village preacher's modest mansion rose.
A man he was to all the country dear,
And passing rich with forty pounds a year;
Remote from towns he ran his godly race,
Nor e'er had changed, nor wished to change his place;
Unpracticed he to fawn, or seek for power,
By doctrines fashioned to the varying hour;
Far other aims his heart had learnt to prize,
More skilled to raise the wretched than to rise.
His house was known to all the vagrant train,
He chid their wanderings, but relieved their pain;
The long-remembered beggar was his guest,
Whose beard descending swept his aged breast;
The ruined spendthrift, now no longer proud,
Claimed kindred there, and had his claims allowed;
The broken soldier, kindly bade to stay,
Sat by his fire, and talked the night away:
Wept o'er his wounds, or tales of sorrow done,
Shouldered his crutch, and showed how fields were
            won
Pleased with his guests, the good man learned to glow,
And quite forgot their vices in their woe;
Careless their merits or their faults to scan,
His pity gave ere charity began.
        Thus to relieve the wretched was his pride,
And e'en his failings leaned to virtue's side;
But in his duty prompt at every call,
He watched and wept, he prayed and felt for all;
And, as a bird each fond endearment tries,
To tempt its new-fledged offspring to the skies,
He tried each art, reproved each dull delay,
Allured to brighter worlds, and led the way.
        Beside the bed where parting life was laid,
And sorrow, guilt and pain by turns dismayed,
The reverend champion stood. At his control,
Despair and anguish fled the struggling soul;

Comfort came down the trembling wretch to raise,
And his last faltering accents whispered praise.
  At church with meek and unaffected grace,
His looks adorned the venerable place;
Truth from his lips prevailed with double sway,
And fools who came to scoff, remained to pray.
The service past, around the pious man,
With steady zeal, each honest rustic ran;
E'en children followed with endearing wile,
And plucked his gown to share the good man's smile;
His ready smile a parent's warmth exprest;
Their welfare pleased him, and their cares distrest.
To them his heart, his love, his griefs were given,
But all his serious thoughts had rest in heaven.
As some tall cliff that lifts its awful form,
Swells from the vale, and midway leaves the storm,
Though round its breast the rolling clouds are spread,
Eternal sunshine settles on his head.
  Beside yon straggling fence that skirts the way,
With blossomed furze unprofitably gay,
There, in his noisy mansion, skilled to rule,
The village master taught his little school:
A man severe he was, and stern to view,
I knew him well, and every truant knew;
Well had the boding tremblers learned to trace
The day's disasters in his morning face;
Full well they laughed with counterfeited glee
At all his jokes, for many a joke had he;
Full well the busy whisper circling round,
Conveyed the dismal tidings when he frowned:
Yet he was kind, or if severe in aught,
The love he bore to learning was in fault;
The village all declared how much he knew,
'Twas certain he could write and cipher too;
Lands he could measure, terms and tides presage,
And e'en the story ran – that he could gauge:
In arguing too, the parson owned his skill,
And e'en though vanquished, he could argue still;
While words of learned length, and thund'ring sound,

Amazed the gazing rustics ranged around;
And still they gazed, and still the wonder grew,
That one small head could carry all he knew.
But passed is all his fame. The very spot
Where many a time he triumphed, is forgot.

O luxury! thou curst by Heaven's decree,
How ill-exchanged are things like these for thee;
How do thy potions, with insidious joy,
Diffuse their pleasures only to destroy!
Kingdoms by thee, to sickly greatness grown,
Boast of a florid vigour not their own:
At every draught more large and large they grow
A bloated mass of rank, unwieldy woe;
Till sapped their strength, and every part unsound,
Down, down, they sink, and spread a ruin round.

E'en now the devastation is begun,
And half the business of destruction done;
E'en now, methinks, as pondering here I stand,
I see the rural virtues leave the land.
Down where yon anchoring vessel spreads the sail,
That idly waiting flaps with every gale,
Downward they move, a melancholy band,
Pass from the shore, and darken all the strand.
Contented toil, and hospitable care,
And kind connubial tenderness are there;
And piety with wishes placed above,
And steady loyalty, and faithful love.

Oliver Goldsmith

Lament for the Death of Eoghan Ruadh O'Neill

'Did they dare, did they dare, to slay Eoghan Ruadh
      O'Neill?'
'Yes, they slew with poison him they feared to meet
      with steel.'
'May God wither up their hearts! May their blood
      cease to flow!
May they walk in living death, who poisoned Eoghan
      Ruadh!'

'Though it break my heart to hear, say again the bitter
      words.'
'From Derry, against Cromwell, he marched to
      measure swords;
But the weapon of the Saxon met him on his way,
And he died at Cloch Uachtar, upon Saint Leonard's
      day.'

'Sagest in the council was he, kindest in the hall:
Sure we never won a battle – 'twas Eoghan won them
      all.
Had he lived – had he lived – our dear country had
      been free;
But he's dead, but he's dead, and 'tis slaves we'll ever
      be.

'O'Farrell and Clanricarde, Preston and Red Hugh,
Audley and MacMahon – ye are valiant, wise and true;
But – what, what are ye all to our darling who is gone?
The Rudder of our ship was he, our Castle's corner-
      stone!

'We thought you would not die – we were sure you
      would not go,

And leave us in our utmost need to Cromwell's cruel
      blow –
Sheep without a shepherd, when the snow shuts out
      the sky –
Oh! why did you leave us Eoghan? Why did you die?'

Thomas Davis

Abbey Assaroe

Grey, grey is Abbey Assaroe, by Belashanny town.
It has neither door nor window, the walls are broken
      down;
The carven stones lie scattered in briar and nettle-bed;
The only feet are those that come at burial of the dead.

A little rocky rivulet runs murmuring to the tide,
Singing a song of ancient days, in sorrow, not in pride;
The boor-tree and the lightsome ash across the portals
      grow,
And heaven itself is now the roof of Abbey Assaroe.

It looks beyond the harbour-stream to Gulban
      mountain blue;
It hears the voice of Erna's fall – Atlantic breakers too;
High ships go sailing past it; the sturdy clank of oars
Brings in the salmon-boat to haul a net upon the
      shores.

And this way to the home-creek, when the summer
      day is done,
Slow sculls the weary fisherman across the setting sun;
While green with corn is Sheegus Hill, his cottage
      white below;
But grey at every season is Abbey Assaroe.

William Allingham

Ode

We are the music-makers,
And we are the dreamer of dreams,
Wandering by lone sea-breakers,
And sitting by desolate streams; –
World-losers and world-forsakers,
On whom the pale moon gleams:
Yet we are the movers and shakers
Of the world for ever, it seems.

With wonderful deathless ditties
We build up the world's great cities
And out of a fabulous story
We fashion an empire's glory:
One man with a dream, at pleasure,
Shall go forth and conquer a crown;
And three with a new song's measure
Can trample a kingdom down.

We, in the ages lying
In the buried past of the earth,
Built Nineveh with our sighing,
And Babel itself in our mirth;
And o'erthrew them with prophesying
To the old of the new world's worth;
For each age is a dream that is dying,
Or one that is coming to birth.

Arthur O'Shaughnessy

Sweet Sorrow

Hy-Brazil – the Isle of the Blest

On the ocean that hollows the rocks where ye dwell,
A shadowy land has appear'd as they tell;
Men thought it a region of sunshine and rest,
And they call'd it 'O Brazil – the Isle of the Blest'.
From year unto year, on the ocean's blue rim,
The beautiful spectre show'd lovely and dim;
The golden clouds curtain'd the deep where it lay.
And it look'd like an Eden, away, far away.

A peasant, who heard of the wonderful tale,
In the breeze of the Orient loosen'd his sail;
From Ara, the holy, he turn'd to the west,
For though Ara was holy, O'Brazil was blest.
He heard not the voices that call'd from the shore –
He heard not the rising wind's menacing roar:
Home, kindred, and safety he left on that day,
And he sped to O'Brazil, away, far away!

Morn rose on the deep, and that shadowy Isle
O'er the faint rim of distance reflected its smile;
Noon burn'd on the wave, and that shadowy shore
Seem'd lovelily distant, and faint as before:
Lone evening came down on the wanderer's track,
And to Ara again he look'd timidly back;
Oh! far on the verge of the ocean it lay,
Yet the Isle of the Blest was away, far away!

Rash dreamer, return! O ye winds of the main,
Bear him back to his old peaceful Ara again!
Rash fool! for a vision of fanciful bliss
To barter the calm life of labour and peace!
The warning of reason was spoken in vain,
He never revisited Ara again;
Night fell on the deep, amidst tempest and spray,
And he died on the waters, away, far away!

To you, gentle friends, need I pause to reveal
The lessons of prudence my verses conceal;
How the phantom of pleasure seen distant in youth,
Oft lures a weak heart from the circle of truth.
All lovely it seems, like that shadowy isle,
And the eye of the wisest is caught by its smile;
But ah! for the heart it has tempted to stray
From the sweet home of duty, away, far away!

Poor friendless adventurer! vainly might he
Look back to green Ara along the wild sea;
But the wanderer's heart has a Guardian above,
Who, though erring, remembers the child of His love.
Oh, who at the proffer of safety would spurn,
When all that He asks is the will to return;
To follow a phantom, from day unto day,
And die in the tempest, away, far away!

Gerald Griffin

My Own Country

Pure was the breeze that fanned my cheek
As o'er Knockmanny's brow I went;
When every lonely dell could speak
In airy music vision-sent.
False world, I hate thy cares and thee,
I hate the treacherous haunts of men;
Give back my early life to me,
Give back to me my mountain glen.

How light my youthful visions shone
When spanned by Fancy's radiant form!
But now the glittering bow is gone
And leaves me but the cloud and storm.
With wasted form and cheek all pale,

With heart long seared by grief and pain,
Dunroe, I'll seek thy native vale,
And tread my mountain glens again.

William Carleton

The Song of Fionnuala

Silent, oh Moyle, be the roar of thy water,
Break not, ye breezes, your chain of repose,
While, murmuring mournfully, Lir's lonely daughter
Tells to the night-star her tale of woes.
When shall the swan, her death-note singing,
Sleep, with wings in darkness furled?
When will heaven, its sweet bell ringing,
Call my spirit from this stormy world!

Sadly, Oh Moyle, to the winter-wave weeping,
Fate bids me languish long ages away;
Yet still in her darkness doth Erin lie sleeping,
Still doth the pure light its dawning delay.
When will that day-star, mildly springing,
Warm our isle with peace and love?
When will heaven, its sweet bell ringing,
Call my spirit to the fields above.

Thomas Moore

The Faithful Light

There's a light in the cottage window –
It shines far over the vale;
The sun is gone and the day is done
And the stars are few and pale.

Only a farthing rushlight,
With a feeble flickering ray –
'Twill gleam and wane in that window-pane
Till wears the night away.

A woman sits in the cottage,
And weeps and tends the light;
Her loving care has placed her there
To glimmer the livelong night.

For one to sea went sailing,
And one will sure come back;
The light must burn till he return
By the lonely beaten track.

He comes not over the mountain,
He comes not across the vale;
The beacon-light keeps burning bright,
Though the woman's face is pale.

He lies deep down in the ocean –
But others cross the plain,
And hearts beat high when passing nigh
That light in the window-pane.

They bless the faithful watcher –
The heart that will not break,
The friendly light in the darksome night
That burns for another's sake.

Her face grows paler and paler –
But wanderers reach their home;
Her loving pain is not in vain
Though one will never come.

Rosa Mulholland (Lady Gilbert)

The Wayfarer

The beauty of the world hath made me sad,
This beauty that will pass;
Sometimes my heart hath shaken with great joy
To see a leaping squirrel in a tree,
Or a red lady-bird upon a stalk
Or little rabbits in a field at evening,
Lit by a slanting sun,
Or some green hill where shadows drifted by,
Some quiet hill where mountainy men hath sown
And soon would reap, near to the gate of Heaven;
Or children with bare feet upon the sands
Of some ebbed sea, or playing on the streets
Of little towns in Connacht,
Things young and happy.
And then my heart hath told me:
These will pass,
Will pass and change, will die and be no more,
Things bright and green, things young and happy;
And I have gone upon my way
Sorrowful.

Padraic H Pearse

Caoch O'Leary

One winter's day, long, long ago,
When I was a little fellow,
A piper wandered to the door,
Grey-headed, blind and yellow;
And oh! how glad was my young heart,
Though earth and sky looked dreary,
To see the stranger and his dog –
Poor 'Pinch' and Caoch O'Leary.

And when he stowed away his 'bag',
Cross-barred with green and yellow,
I thought and said 'In Ireland's ground
There's not so fine a fellow.'
And then he stroked my flaxen hair,
And cried, 'God mark my deary!'
And how I wept when he said 'farewell',
And thought of Caoch O'Leary!

Well – twenty summers had gone past,
And June's red sun was sinking,
When I, a man, sat by my door,
Of twenty sad things thinking.
A little dog came up the way,
His gait was slow and weary,
And at his tail a lame man limped –
'Twas 'Pinch' and Caoch O'Leary!

'God's blessing here!' the wanderer cried,
'Far, far be hell's black viper;
Does anybody hereabouts
Remember Caoch the Piper?'
With swelling heart I grasped his hand;
The old man murmured 'Deary,
Are you the silky-headed child
That loved poor Caoch O'Leary?'

'Yes, yes,' I said – the wanderer wept
As if his heart was breaking –
'And where, *a vic machree,*' he sobbed,
'Is all the merry-making
I found here twenty years ago?'
'My tale,' I sighed, 'might weary;
Enough to say – there's none but me
To welcome Caoch O'Leary.'

'Vo, vo, vo!' the old man cried,
And wrung his hands in sorrow,
'Pray let me in, *astore machree,*
And I'll go home tomorrow.
My peace is made; I'll gladly leave
This world so cold and dreary;
And you shall keep my pipes and dog,
And pray for Caoch O'Leary.'

With 'Pinch' I watched his bed that night;
Next day his wish was granted:
He died; and Father James was brought,
And Requiem Mass was chanted.
The neighbours came; we dug his grave
Near Eily, Kate and Mary,
And there he sleeps his last, sweet sleep:
God rest you! Caoch O'Leary.

John Keegan

The Old Woman of the Roads

Oh to have a little house!
To own the hearth and stool and all!
The heaped-up sods upon the fire,
The pile of turf against the wall!

82

To have a clock with weights and chains,
And pendulum swinging up and down!
A dresser filled with shining delph,
Speckled with white and blue and brown!

I could be busy all the day
Cleaning and sweeping hearth and floor,
And fixing on their shelf again
My white and blue and speckled store!

I could be quiet there at night
Beside the fire and by myself,
Sure of a bed and loath to leave
The ticking clock and the shining delph!

Och! but I'm weary of mist and dark,
And roads where there's never a house nor bush,
And tired I am of bog and road,
And the crying wind and the lonesome hush!

And I am praying to God on high,
And I am praying Him night and day,
For a little house – a house of my own –
Out of the wind and the rain's way.

Padraic Colum

The Ballad of Father Gilligan

The old priest Peter Gilligan
Was weary night and day;
For half his flock were in their beds,
Or under green sods lay.

Once while he nodded on a chair,
At the moth-hour of the eve,

Another poor man sent for him,
And he began to grieve.

'I have no rest, nor joy, nor peace,
For people die and die';
And after cried he, 'God forgive!
My body spake, not I!'

He knelt, and leaning on the chair
He prayed and fell asleep;
And the moth-hour went from the fields,
And stars began to peep.

They slowly into millions grew,
And leaves shook in the wind;
And God covered the world with shade,
And whispered to mankind.

Upon the time of sparrow chirp
When the moths came once more,
The old priest Peter Gilligan
Stood upright on the floor.

'Mavrone, mavrone! the man has died,
While I slept on the chair';
He roused his horse out of its sleep,
And rode with little care.

He rode now as he never rode,
By rocky lane and fen;
The sick man's wife opened the door;
'Father, you come again!'

'And is the poor man dead?' he cried.
'He died an hour ago.'
The old priest Peter Gilligan
In grief swayed to and fro.

'When you were gone, he turned and died

As merry as a bird.'
The old priest Peter Gilligan
He knelt him at that word.

'He who hath made the night of stars
For souls who tire and bleed,
Sent one of His great angels down
To help me in my need.

'He who is wrapped in purple robes,
With planets in His care,
Had pity on the least of things
Asleep upon a chair.'

W B Yeats

Unlaboured Fields

The silence of unlaboured fields
Lies like a judgment in the air:
A human voice is never heard:
The sighing grass is everywhere –
The sighing grass, the shadowed sky,
The cattle crying wearily.

Where are the lowland people gone?
Where are the sun-dark faces now?
The love that kept the quiet hearth,
The strength that held the speeding plough?
Grasslands and lowing herds are good,
But better human flesh and blood!

Joseph Campbell

The House with Nobody In It

Whenever I walk to Suffern along the Erie track
I go by a poor old farmhouse, with its shingles broken
    and black,
I suppose I've passed it a hundred times, but I always
    stop for a minute
And look at that house, the tragic house, the house
    with nobody in it.

This house on the road to Suffern needs a dozen panes
    of glass,
And somebody ought to weed the walk and take a
    scythe to the grass.
It needs new painting and shingles, and the vines
    should be trimmed and tied;
But what it needs the most of all is some people living
    inside.

If I had a lot of money and all my debts were paid
I'd put a gang of men to work with brush and saw and
    spade.
I'd buy that place and fix it up the way it used to be,
And I'd find some people who wanted a home and
    give it to them for free.

Now, a new house standing empty, with staring
    window and door,
Looks idle, perhaps and foolish, like a hat on its block
    in the store.
But there's nothing mournful about it; it cannot be sad
    and lone
For the lack of something within it that it has never
    known.

But a house that has done what a house should do, a
    house that has sheltered life,

That has put its loving wooden arms around a man
and his wife,
A house that has echoed a baby's laugh and held up
his stumbling feet,
Is the saddest sight, when it's left alone, that ever your
eyes could meet.

So whenever I go to Suffern along the Erie track
I never go by the empty house without stopping and
looking back;
Yet it hurts me to look at the crumbling roof and the
shutters falling apart,
For I can't help thinking the poor old house is a house
with a broken heart.

Joyce Kilmer

Years of Exile

'Tis, it is the Shannon's Stream

'Tis, it is the Shannon's stream,
Brightly glancing, brightly glancing!
See, oh see the ruddy beam
Upon its waters dancing!
To see old Shannon's face again,
Oh, the bliss entrancing!
Hail, our own majestic stream
Flowing ever, flowing ever,
Silent in the morning beam,
Our beloved river!

Fling the rocky portals wide,
Western ocean, western ocean!
Bend, ye hills, on either side,
In solemn, deep devotion!
While before the rising gales,
On his heaving surface sails
Half the wealth of Erin's vales
With undulating motion.
Hail, our own beloved stream,
Flowing ever, flowing ever,
Silent in the morning beam,
Our own majestic river!

Gerald Griffin

The Wind that Shakes the Barley

There's music in my heart all day,
I hear it late and early,
It comes from fields are far away,
The wind that shakes the barley.

Above the uplands drenched with dew
The sky hangs soft and pearly,
An emerald world is listening to
The wind that shakes the barley.

Above the bluest mountain crest
The lark is singing rarely,
It rocks the singer into rest,
The wind that shakes the barley.

Oh, still through summers and through springs
It calls me late and early.
Come home, come home, come home, it sings,
The wind that shakes the barley.

Katherine Tynan

As Slow Our Ship

As slow our ship her foamy track
Against the wind was cleaving,
Her trembling pennant still look'd back
To that dear isle 'twas leaving.
So loath we part from all we love,
From all the links that bind us;

So turn our hearts, as on we rove,
To those we've left behind us!

When, round the bowl, of vanish'd years
We talk with joyous seeming –
With smiles that might as well be tears,
So faint, so sad their beaming;
While memory brings us back again
Each early tie that twined us,
Oh, sweet's the cup that circles then
To those we've left behind us!

And when, in other climes, we meet
Some isle or vale enchanting,
Where all looks flowery, wild and sweet,
And nought but love is wanting;
We think how great had been our bliss
If Heaven had but assign'd us
To live and die in scenes like this,
With some we've left behind us!

As travellers oft look back at eve
When eastward darkly going,
To gaze upon that light they leave
Still faint behind them glowing –
So, when the close of pleasure's day
To gloom hath near consign'd us,
We turn to catch one fading ray
Of joy that's left behind us.

Thomas Moore

The Shandon Bells

With deep affection
And recollection
I often think of
Those Shandon Bells,
Whose sound so wild would,
In days of childhood,
Fling round my cradle
Their magic spells.
On this I ponder
Where'er I wander
And thus grow fonder,
Sweet Cork of thee;
With the bells of Shandon
That sound so grand on
The pleasant waters
Of the river Lee.

I've heard bells chiming
Full many a clime in,
Tolling sublime in
Cathedral shrine,
While at a glib rate
Brass tongues would vibrate –
But all their music
Spoke naught like thine;
For memory dwelling
On each proud swelling
Of the belfry knelling
Its bold notes free,
Made the bells of Shandon
Sound far more grand on
The pleasant waters
Of the river Lee.

I've heard bells tolling

Old 'Adrian's Mole' in
Their thunder rolling
From the Vatican,
And Cymbals glorious
Swinging uproarious
In the glorious turrets
Of Notre Dame;
But thy sounds were sweeter
Than the dome of Peter
Flings o'er the Tiber,
Pealing solemnly; –
O! the bells of Shandon
Sound far more grand on
The pleasant waters
Of the river Lee.

There's a bell in Moscow,
While on tower and kiosk O!
In Saint Sophia
The Turkman gets,
And loud in air
Calls men to prayer
From the tapering summit
Of tall minarets.
Such empty phantom
I freely grant them;
But there is an anthem
More dear to me –
'Tis the bells of Shandon,
That sound so grand on
The pleasant waters
Of the river Lee.

Father Prout (F S Mahony)

Lough Bray

A little lonely moorland lake,
Its waters brown and cool and deep –
The cliff, the hills behind it, make
A picture for my heart to keep.

For rock and heather, wave and strand,
Wore tints I rarely saw them wear;
The June sunshine was o'er the land;
Before, 'twas never half so fair!

The amber ripples sang all day,
And singing spilled their crowns of white
Upon the beach, in thin pale spray
That streaked the sober strand with light.

The amber ripples sang their song,
When suddenly from far o'erhead
A lark's pure voice mixed with the throng
Of lovely things about us spread.

Some flowers were there, so near the brink
Their shadows in the wave were thrown;
While mosses green and grey and pink,
Grew thickly round each smooth dark stone.

And over all the summer sky;
Shut out the town we left behind;
'Twas joy to stand in silence by,
One bright chain linking mind to mind.

Oh, little lonely mountain spot!
Your place within my heart will be
Apart from all Life's busy lot
A true, sweet, solemn memory.

Rose Kavanagh

An Old Tune

'Mongst the green Irish hills I love dearly,
At the close of the bright summer day,
I heard an old tune lilted clearly,
That soothed half my sorrows away.
And far o'er the wide-rolling ocean
Methinks I am hearing it now,
As a farewell of tender emotion –
'The Pretty Girl milking her cow'.

Next day was the last look of Erin;
'Twas almost like death to depart;
And since, in my foreign wayfaring,
That tune's like a thread round my heart.
Still back to the dear old Green Island
It draws me, I cannot tell how,
The whisper in music of my land –
'The Pretty Girl milking her cow'.

William Allingham

Isle of Beauty

Shades of evening, close not o'er us,
Leave our lonely bark awhile;
Morn, alas! will not restore us
Yonder dim and distant isle.
Still my fancy can discover
Sunny spots where friends may dwell;
Darker shadows round us hover,
Isle of Beauty, fare thee well!

'Tis the hour when happy faces

Smile around the taper's light;
Who will fill our vacant places?
Who will sing our songs tonight?
Through the mist that floats above us
Faintly sounds the vesper-bell,
Like a sound from those who love us,
Breathing fondly fare thee well.

When the waves are round us breaking,
As I pace the deck alone,
And my eye is vainly seeking
Some green leaf to rest upon;
When on that dear land I ponder,
Where my old companions dwell,
Absence makes the heart grow fonder,
Isle of Beauty, fare thee well!

Thomas Haynes Bayly

After Aughrim

She said, 'They gave me of their best,
They lived, they gave their lives for me;
I tossed them to the howling waste,
And flung them to the foaming sea.'

She said, 'I never gave them aught,
Not mine the power, if mine the will;
I let them starve, I let them bleed –
They bled and starved, and loved me still.'

She said, 'Ten times they fought for me,
Ten times they strove with might and main,
Ten times I saw them beaten down,
Ten times they rose, and fought again.'

She said, 'I never called them sons,
I almost ceased to breathe their name,
Then caught it echoing down the wind,
Blown backwards from the lips of Fame.'

She said, 'Not mine, not mine that fame;
Far over sea, far over land,
Cast forth like rubbish from my shores,
They won it yonder, sword in hand.'

She said, 'God knows they owe me nought,
I tossed them to the foaming sea,
I tossed them to the howling waste,
Yet still their love comes home to me.'

Emily Lawless

The Lake Isle of Inisfree

I will arise and go now, and go to Inisfree,
And a small cabin build there, of clay and wattles
    made;
Nine bean-rows will I have there, a hive for the
    honey bee,
And live alone in the bee-loud glade.

And I shall have some peace there, for peace comes
    dropping slow,
Dropping from the veils of the morning to where
    the cricket sings;
There midnight's all a glimmer, and noon a purple
    glow,
And evening full of the linnet's wings.

I will arise and go now, for always night and day

I hear lake water lapping with low sounds by the
    shore;
While I stand on the roadway, or on the pavements
    grey,
I hear it in the deep heart's core.

W B Yeats

Irish Skies

In London here the streets are grey,
and grey the sky above;
I wish I were in Ireland to see the skies
I love –
Pearl cloud, buff cloud, the colour of a dove.

All day I travel English streets, but in
my dreams I tread
The far Glencullen road and see
the soft sky overhead,
Grey clouds, white clouds, the wind has
    shepherded.

At night the London lamps shine bright,
but what are they to me?
I've seen the moonlight in Glendhu,
the stars above Glenchree –
The lamps of heaven give light enough for me.

The city in the winter time put on
a shroud of smoke,
But the sky above the Three Rock was blue
as Mary's cloak,
Ruffled like dove's wings when the wind awoke.

I dream I see the Wicklow hills
by evening sunlight kissed,

And every glen and valley there
brimful of radiant mist –
The jewelled sky topaz and amethyst.

I wake to see the London streets,
the sombre sky above,
God's blessing on the far-off roads,
and on the skies I love –
Pearl feather, grey feather, wings of dove.

Winifred M Letts

The Exile's Return

Glory to God, but there it is –
The dawn on the hills of Ireland!
God's angels lifting the night's black veil
From the fair, sweet face of my sireland!
O Ireland! isn't it grand you look –
Like a bride in her rich adorning!
With all the pent-up love of my heart
I bid you the top of the morning!

This one short hour pays lavishly back
For many a year of mourning;
I'd almost venture another flight,
There's so much joy in returning –
Watching out for the hallowed shore,
All other attractions scorning;
O Ireland! don't you hear me shout?
I bid you the top of the morning.

See how on Cliodhna's shelving strand
The surges are grandly beating,
And Kerry is pushing her headlands out
To give us the kindly greeting!

In to the shore the sea-birds fly
On pinions that know no drooping,
And out from the cliffs, with welcome charged,
A million waves come trooping.

O kindly, generous, Irish land,
So loyal and fair and loving!
No wonder the wandering Celt should think
And dream of you in this roving.
The alien home may have gems of gold,
Shadows may never have gloomed it;
But the heart will sigh for the absent land
Where the love-light first illumed it.

And doesn't old Cobh look charming there,
Watching the wild waves' motion,
Leaning her back up against the hills,
And the tip of her toes in the ocean.
I wonder I don't hear the Shandon bells –
Ah! maybe their chiming's over,
For it's many a year since I began
The life of a western rover.

For forty summers, *a stor mo chroi*,
Those hills I now feast my eyes on
Ne'er met my vision save when they rose
Over memory's dim horizon.
E'en so, 'twas grand and fair they seemed
In the landscape spread before me;
But dreams are dreams, and my eyes would ope
To see Texas skies still o'er me.

Oh! often upon the Texans plains,
When the day and the chase were over,
My thoughts would fly o'er the weary wave,
And around the coast-line hover;
And the prayer would rise that some future day –
All danger and doubt scorning –
I'd help to win for my native land

The light of young Liberty's morning!

Now fuller and truer the shoreline shows –
Was ever a scene so splendid?
I feel the breath of the Munster breeze,
Thank God that my exile's ended!
Old scenes, old songs, old friends again,
The vale and the cot I was born in –
O Ireland! up from my heart of hearts,
I bid you the top of the morning!

John Locke

Love of Country

My Land

She is a rich and rare land,
Oh she's a fresh and fair land;
She is a dear and rare land,
This native land of mine.

No men than hers are braver,
Her women's hearts ne'er waver;
I'd freely die to save her,
And think my lot divine.

She's not a dull or cold land,
No, she's a warm and bold land,
Oh, she's a true and old land,
This native land of mine.

Could beauty ever guard her,
And virtue still reward her,
No foe would cross her border –
No friend within it pine.

Oh, she's a fresh and fair land,
Oh, she's a true and rare land;
Yes she's a rare and fair land,
This native land of mine.

Thomas Davis

Lament for Thomas MacDonagh

He shall not hear the bittern cry
In the wild sky, where he is lain,
Nor voices of the sweeter birds
Above the wailing of the rain.

Nor shall he know when loud March blows
Thro' slanting snows her fanfare shrill,
Blowing to flame the golden cup
Of many an upset daffodil.

But when the Dark Cow leaves the moor
And pastures poor with greedy weeds
Perhaps he'll hear her low at morn,
Lifting her horn in pleasant meads.

Francis Ledwidge

A Ballad of Athlone

Does any man dream that a Gael can fear? –
Of a thousand deeds let him learn but one!
The Shannon swept onward, broad and clear,
Between the leaguers and broad Athlone.

'Break down the bridge!' Six warriors rushed
Through the storm of shot and the storm of shell:
With late but certain victory flushed,
The grim Dutch gunners eyed them well.

They wrenched at the planks 'mid a hail of fire:
They fell in death, their work half done:
The bridge stood fast; and nigh and nigher

The foe swarmed darkly, densely on.

'Oh who for Erin will strike a stroke?
Who hurl yon planks where the waters roar?'
Six warriors forth from their comrades broke,
And flung them upon that bridge once more.

Again at the rocking planks they dashed;
And four dropped dead; and two remained:
The huge beams groaned and the arch down-
  crashed; –
Two stalwart swimmers the margin gained.

St Ruth in his stirrups stood up and cried:
'I have seen no deed like that in France!'
With a toss of his head, Sarsfield replied,
'They had luck, the dogs! 'Twas a merry chance!'

Oh, many a year upon Shannon's side
They sang upon moor and they sang upon heath
Of the twain that had breasted the raging tide,
And the ten that shook bloody hands with Death!

Aubrey de Vere

Michael Dwyer

The soldiers searched the valley, and towards the
  dawn of day
Discovered where the outlaws, the dauntless rebels,
  lay.
Around the little cottage they formed into a ring
And called out: 'Michael Dwyer! surrender to the
  King'.

Thus answered Michael Dwyer: 'Into this house we
  came

Unasked by those who own it – they cannot be to
    blame.
Then let these peaceful people unquestioned pass you
    through,
And when they're placed in safety, I'll tell you what
    we'll do.'

'Twas done. 'And now,' said Dwyer, 'your work you
    may begin:
You are a hundred outside – we're only four within.
We've heard your haughty summons, and this is our
    reply –
We're true United Irishmen, we'll fight until we die.'

Then burst the war's red lightning, then poured the
    leaden rain,
The hills around re-echoed the thunder peals again.
The soldiers falling round him brave Dwyer sees with
    pride;
But, ah! one gallant comrade is wounded by his side.

Yet there are three remaining good battle still to do:
Their hands are strong and steady, their aim is quick
    and true –
But hark that furious shouting the savage soldiers
    raise!
The house is fired around them; the roof is in a blaze!

And brighter every moment the lurid flame arose,
And louder swelled the laughter and cheering of their
    foes;
Then spake the brave MacAllister, the weak and
    wounded man:
'You can escape my comrades, and this shall be your
    plan:

'Place in my hands a musket, then lie upon the floor:
I'll stand before the soldiers and open wide the door;
They'll pour into my bosom the fire of their array;

Then, whilst their guns are empty, dash through them
          and away.'

He stood before his foemen, revealed amidst the flame;
From out their levelled pieces the wished-for volley
          came;
Up sprang the three survivors for whom the hero died,
But only Michael Dwyer broke through the ranks
          outside.

He baffled his pursuers, who followed like the wind;
He swam the river Slaney and left them far behind;
But many an English soldier he promised should soon
          fall
For these, his gallant comrades, who died in wild
          Imaal.

T D Sullivan

Dark Rosaleen

O, my Dark Rosaleen,
Do not sigh, do not weep!
The priests are on the ocean green,
They march along the deep.
There's wine ... from the royal Pope,
Upon the ocean green;
And Spanish ale shall give you hope,
My Dark Rosaleen!
My own Rosaleen!
Shall glad your heart, shall give you hope,
Shall give you health, and help, and hope,
My Dark Rosaleen!

Over hills, and through dales,
Have I roamed for your sake;

All yesterday I sailed with sails
On river and on lake.
The Erne, at its highest flood,
I dashed across unseen,
For there was lightning in my blood,
My Dark Rosaleen!
My own Rosaleen!
O! there was lightning in my blood,
Red lightning lightened through my blood,
My Dark Rosaleen!

Woe and pain, pain and woe,
Are my lot, night and noon,
To see your bright face clouded so,
Like to the mournful moon.
But yet, will I rear your throne
Again in golden sheen;
'Tis you shall reign, shall reign alone,
My Dark Rosaleen!
My own Rosaleen!
'Tis you shall have the golden throne,
'Tis you shall reign, and reign alone,
My Dark Rosaleen!

I could scale the blue air,
I could plough the high hills,
Oh, I could kneel all night in prayer,
To heal your many ills!
And one beamy smile from you
Would float like light between
My toils and me, my own, my true,
My Dark Rosaleen!
My fond Rosaleen!
Would give me life and soul anew,
A second life, a soul anew,
My Dark Rosaleen!

O! the Erne shall run red
With redundance of blood,

The earth shall rock beneath our tread,
And flames wrap hill and wood,
And gun-peal, and slogan cry,
Wake many a glen serene.
Ere you shall fade, ere you shall die,
My Dark Rosaleen!
My own Rosaleen!
The Judgment Hour must first be nigh,
Ere you can fade, ere you can die,
My Dark Rosaleen!

James Clarence Mangan

She is Far from the Land

She is far from the land where her young hero sleeps,
And lovers are round her sighing;
But coldly she turns from their gaze and weeps,
For her heart is in his grave lying.

She sings the wild song of her dear native plains,
Every note which he loved awaking; –
Ah! little they think, who delight in their strains,
How the heart of the Minstrel is breaking.

He had lived for his love, for his country he died,
They were all that to life had entwined him;
Nor soon shall the tears of his country be dried,
Nor long will his love stay behind him.

Oh! make her a grave where the sunbeams rest
When they promise a glorious morrow;
They'll shine o'er her sleep, like a smile from the west,
From her own loved island of sorrow.

Thomas Moore

The Burial of Sir John Moore

Not a drum was heard, not a funeral note,
As his corpse to the ramparts we hurried;
Not a soldier discharged his farewell shot
O'er the grave of our hero we buried.

We buried him darkly at dead of night,
The sods with our bayonets turning;
By the struggling moonbeams misty light
And the lantern dimly burning.

No useless coffin enclosed his breast,
Not in sheet or in shroud we wound him;
But he lay like a warrior taking his rest,
With his martial cloak around him.

Few and short were the prayers we said,
And we spoke not a word of sorrow;
But we steadfastly stared on the face that was dead,
And we bitterly thought of the morrow.

We thought as we hollow'd his narrow bed
And smoothed down his lonely pillow,
That the foe and the stranger would tread o'er his
    head,
And we far away on the billow!

Lightly they'll talk of the spirit that's gone
And in his cold ashes upbraid him –
But little he'll reck, if they let him sleep on
In the grave where a Briton laid him.

But half of our heavy task was done
When the clock struck the hour for departing:
And we heard the distant and random gun
That the foe was sullenly firing.

Slowly and sadly we laid him down,
From the field of his fame fresh and gory;
We carved not a line, and we raised not a stone,
But we left him alone with his glory.

Charles Wolfe

Let Me Carry Your Cross for Ireland, Lord!

Let me carry your Cross for Ireland, Lord!
The hour of her trial draws near,
And the pangs and the pains of the sacrifice
May be borne by comrades dear.
But, Lord, take me from the offering throng,
There are many far less prepared,
Though anxious and all as they are to die
That Ireland may be spared.

Let me carry your Cross for Ireland, Lord!
My cares in this world are few,
And few are the tears will fall for me
When I go on my way to You.
Spare, oh spare to their loved ones dear
The brother, the son and the sire;
That the cause we love may never die
In the land of our heart's desire!

Let me carry your Cross for Ireland, Lord!
Let me suffer the pain and shame.
I bow my head to their rage and hate,
And I take on myself the blame.
Let them do with my body whate'er they will,
My spirit I offer to You,
That the faithful few who heard her call

May be spared to Roisin Dubh.

Let me carry your Cross for Ireland, Lord!
For Ireland weak with tears,
For the aged man of the clouded brow,
And the child of tender years;
For the empty homes of her golden plains;
For the hopes of her future, too!
Let me carry your Cross for Ireland, Lord!
For the cause of Roisin Dubh.

Thomas Ashe

The March to Kinsale

O'er many a river bridged with ice,
Through many a vale with snow-drifts dumb,
Past quaking fen and precipice
The Princes of the North are come!

Lo, these are they that year by year
Roll'd back the tide of England's war; –
Rejoice, Kinsale! thy help is near!
That wondrous winter march is o'er.

And thus they sang, 'Tomorrow morn
Our eyes shall rest upon the foe:
Roll on swift night, in silence borne,
And blow, thou breeze of sunrise, blow!'

Blithe as a boy on marched the host,
With droning pipe and clear-voiced harp;
At last above that southern coast
Rang out their war-steeds' whinny sharp:

And up the sea-salt slopes they wound,

And airs once more of ocean quaff'd:
Those frosty woods the rocks that crown'd
As though May touched them, waved and laugh'd.

And thus they sang, 'Tomorrow morn
Our eyes shall rest upon our foe
Roll on, swift night, in silence borne,
And blow, thou breeze of sunrise, blow!'

Aubrey de Vere

John Mitchel's Farewell to His Country

I am a true born Irishman, John Mitchel is my name,
When first I joined my countrymen from Newry town I
    came;
I laboured hard both day and night to free my native
    land,
And for that I was transported unto Van Dieman's
    land.

When first I joined my countrymen it was in forty-two,
And what did happen after that I'll quickly tell to you;
I raised the standard of Repeal, I gloried in the deed,
I vowed to Heaven I ne'er would rest till Ireland would
    be freed.

Farewell, my gallant comrades, it grieves my heart full
    sore
To think that I must part with you, perhaps for
    evermore.
The love I bear my native land, I know no other crime;
That is the reason I must go unto a foreign clime.

As I lay in iron bounds, before my trial day,
My loving wife came to my cell, and thus to me did
      say –
'Cheer up my gallant husband, undaunted always be,
'Tis better to die a thousand deaths than live in
      slavery.'

I said 'My darling girl, it grieves my heart full sore
To think from you that I must part, perhaps for
      evermore;
Also my friends and relatives, will mourn my sad
      downfall,
But to part from my native land, it grieves me more
      than all.'

I was quickly placed in the dock, still in strong irons
      bound,
Whilst numbers of my countrymen were gathered all
      around;
I was offered then my liberty if I'd deny the cause,
But I'd rather die on a gallows high than suffer tyrant
      laws.

I was placed on board a convict ship without the least
      delay,
For Bermuda's Isle our course was steered, I'll ne'er
      forget the day;
And as I stood upon the deck to take a farewell view,
I shed a tear, but not for fear, my native land, for you.

Adieu, Adieu, to sweet Belfast, likewise to Dublin too,
And to my young and tender babes; alas what will
      they do,
But one request I ask of you, when your liberty you
      gain,
Remember Mitchel, far away, a convict o'er the main.

John Mitchel

My Own Land

This world hath many a glorious land,
Where beauty ever dwells,
Old snow-crowned hills, and rivers grand,
And happy summer dells.

Of these the Poet in his lays,
Loves evermore to tell,
Where heroes died in former days,
Where Freedom's martyrs fell.

But my own land is dearer far,
Than all, where'er they be,
My own land – my own land –
Is all the world to me!

Robert Emmet

Index of First Lines

Acknowledgements

Thanks are due to the following for permission to reprint the material indicated: Simon D Campbell for 'I will go with my Father a-ploughing' and 'The Silence of Unlaboured Fields' by Joseph Campbell; The Trustee of the estate of Padraic Colum for 'The Old Woman of the Roads', 'A Drover' and 'A Cradle Song'; John P Sheridan for 'Timothy Dan', 'Sycamore Tree' and 'And then I Remembered' by John D Sheridan; The Society of Authors on behalf of the copyright owner, Mrs Iris Wise for 'Danny Murphy', 'White Fields' and 'The Snare' by James Stephens

Every effort has been made to trace the owners of the copyright material and it is hoped that no copyright has been infringed. If we have inadvertently infringed any copyright we apologise and will make the necessary correction at the first opportunity.

Between Innocence and Peace: Favourite Poems Of Ireland
Chosen and introduced by Brendan Kennelly

Brendan Kennelly has chosen poems that give him a thrill or a laugh, poems that sing clouds or sunlight into his heart, poems that he is glad to read again and again for a whole host of reasons.

They're all here: sad poems, mad poems, funny poems, lonely poems, poems that demonstrate and celebrate the partitioned culture of Ireland, poems by and about women, poems that tell lies beautifully and truths clumsily, poems that sing the pains and joys of history, that tell of spiritual desolation, physical desire, remorse, love, myth, exile, homesickness, hatred, dreams, prejudice, nightmares, superstition, illness, health, war, religion, disaster and death. And all, all between innocence and peace.

LOVE OF IRELAND: POEMS FROM THE IRISH
Brendan Kennelly

Love of Ireland is a magical collection of translations from the Irish by one of Ireland's leading poets. Here he has captured all of the spontaneity, candour, freshness and emotional fullness of Irish poetry.

BALLADS OF A BOGMAN

Sigerson Clifford

Almost invariable Sigerson Clifford has set his word pictures against the mountain backdrop that edges Dingle Bay from the Laune to the Inney. To visit his Kerry is to go with him along the heathery pathways above Cahirciveen, or to sit with him in the cosy pub. With a rare sense of intimacy he will take you on bare feet through the dew-wet grass of sloping fields before the morning sun tops the shoulder of one of his mountains, or set you down in the scent of the smouldering turf under low rafters as darkly brown as the stout in your glass. In these poems Sigerson Clifford has caught and held the witchery of Kerry.

AROUND THE BOREE LOG
and other verses

John O'Brien

Around the Boree Log is verse that is simple and sincere and lit with kindly understanding of the lives it chronicles.

> *For when the Holy Morning strung*
> *Its beads upon the grass,*
> *You'd see us driving – old and young –*
> *The tall white graceful trees among,*
> *On every road to Mass.*

THE MIDNIGHT COURT
A Dual-Language Book
A new translation by Patrick C. Power

This is a racy, word-rich, bawdy poem – full of uncompromising language and attitudes which have earned it increasing admiration and popularity since it was first composed by Brian Merriman in 1780. The bachelor uninterested in marriage and the aged bone-cold married man, the spouse-hunting lady and the dissatisfied spinster; the celebration of a woman's right to sex and marriage; disapproval of clerical celibacy – all these elements form part of *The Midnight Court*.

The translation supplied with this edition of Merriman's poem is an endeavour to come as near as possible to the rural expression and attitudes which are part and parcel of the original.

FORBHAIS DROMA DÁMHGHÁIRE
The Siege of Knocklong

Seán ó Duinn

Originally part of *The Book of Lismore* this ancient Irish epic (which could be called the *Táin* of Munster) is a marvellous story of magic and fantasy, political influence and vengeance, with a wealth of place-names and curious traditions. The story concerns the march of the high-king Cormac MacAirt, his army and druids, from Tara into Munster for the purpose of forcing Fiacha, King of Munster, to pay taxes.

A Dual-Language Book

THE RED-HAIRED WOMAN
and Other Stories

Sigerson Clifford

'He blamed Red Ellie for his failure to sell. She stood before him on the road that morning, shook her splendid mane of foxy hair at him, and laughed. He should have returned to his house straightaway and waited 'till she left the road. It was what the fishermen always did when they met her. It meant bad luck to meet a red-haired woman when you went fishing or selling. Everyone knew that ...'

'This collection of stories has humour, shrewd observation, sharp wit at times, and the calm sure touch of an accomplished storyteller ... '
From the Introduction by Brendan Kennelly.

Each of 'Sigerson Clifford's delicious tales ... in *The Red-Haired Woman and Other Stories* is a quick, often profound glimpse of Irish life, mostly in the countryside. The characters appear, fall into a bit of trouble and get wherever they're going without a lot of palaver. The simple plots glisten with semi-precious gems of language ...'
James F. Clarity, **The New York Times Book Review**

'Flavoured by the wit and sweetness of the Irish language, this slender volume presents brief affectionate glimpses of Irish country life.'
Leone McDermott, **Booklist**

MY VILLAGE – MY WORLD

John M. Feehan

*This is a book that never palls or drags. It is boisterous
and ribald and I am tempted to say that it is by far the
funniest book I have ever read. It is also an accurate and
revealing history of rural Ireland half a century ago and
more. John M. Feehan writes beautifully throughout. I
love this book.*

From the Foreword by John B. Keane

My Village – My World is a fascinating account of ordinary
people in the countryside. It depicts a way of life that took
thousands of years to evolve and mature and was destroy-
ed in a single generation. As John M. Feehan says 'Nobody
famous ever came from our village. None of its inhabitants
ever achieved great public acclaim ... The people of our
village could be described in government statistics as un-
skilled. That would be a false description. They were all
highly skilled, whether in constructing privies or making
coffins, digging drains or cutting hedges, droving cattle or
tending to stallions ... I do not want to paint a picture of an
idyllic village like Goldsmith's phony one. We had our
sinners as well as our saints ...'

IRISH FAIRY STORIES
for Children

Edmund Leamy

In these stories we read all about the exciting adventures
of Irish children in fairyland. We meet the fairy minstrel,
giants, leprechauns, fairy queens and wonderful talking
animals in Tir na nÓg.

THE CHILDREN'S BOOK OF
IRISH FAIRY TALES

Patricia Dunn

The five exciting stories in this book tell of the mythical,
enchanted origins of Irish landmarks when the country-
side was peopled with good fairies, wicked witches,
gallent heroes and beautiful princesses.

Did you know that there are bright, shimmering lakes
in Killarney concealing submerged castles, mountain
peaks in Wexford created by magic, a dancing bush in
Cork bearing life-saving berries, the remains of a witch in a
Kerry field and deer with silver and golden horns around
Lough Gartan in Donegal?

These stories tell of extraordinary happenings long,
long ago and show that evidence of these exciting events
can still be seen today if you only take the time to look
carefully.